Ragnar Lothbrok

A Biography of Ragnar Lothbrok, A Viking Warrior and King

Table of Contents

Introduction

Thank you for taking the time to pick up this book all about Ragnar Lothbrok.

Ragnar Lothbrok was a legendary Viking warrior and King, who's tales have survived over 1000 years. Though his true existence is still debated to this day, Ragnar has been the inspiration for many books, movies, and even a TV series; Vikings.

In the following chapters you will discover who Ragnar Lothbrok was, and what impact he had on the Viking culture. You will learn about his ruthless war tactics, his fearsome brutality, his lineage, and his legacy.

Also discussed in this book is the Norse Mythology that shaped the bulk of Ragnar's beliefs and motivations for living the way he did.

Once again, thanks for choosing this book! I hope you find learning about Ragnar Lothbrok, the most famous Viking warrior, to be a fascinating journey.

Chapter 1: Who Was Ragnar?

Vikings were Norse seafarers that spoke an Old Norse language. They are known for raiding and trading from their Northern Europe homelands all the way to central and eastern parts of Europe during the 8th to 11th centuries. They had incredible seafaring navigation skills and were characterized by the longship, which is literally a long, narrow ship that is powered by both oars and sails. It is said that Viking activities did eventually branch out into North Africa, the Middle East, Central Asia, and even the Mediterranean, though much less is known about these times than others. They looked to expand their territory by raiding, pillaging, and overtaking cities in areas they felt they could flourish, and it is this dissemination of the Norse culture that eventually developed into areas such as Sweden and Scandinavia.

Modern conceptions of the Vikings picture them as noble savages, which would be a highly romanticized idea compared to what uncovered history and archaeology has told us about the Vikings. This romanticized story of the Vikings emerged in the 18th century and was widely spread and propagated during a 19th-century Viking revival that took place during that time period. But, with the rise of this romanticized story came a highly skewed version in the opposite direction, which painted Vikings as piratical, violent criminals and unwanted adventurers that only traveled to wreak havoc and take lives.

In the records of history that we do have of the Vikings, the earliest recorded raids that involved them are from the 790s. But, it is not until 1066 that the Norman conquest of England, which is commonly known as the Viking Age of Scandinavian history, would begin to cement itself in history. During this time, the Vikings utilized the Baltic and Norwegian Seas in order to travel to the south, and even though they ventured this way they would continue to have a big influence in northern Europe. They had this influence because of how the Normans came to be: Normans were the descendants of Vikings but did not step onto the longships in order to go on conquests, and instead were given feudal over-lordship in areas we now understand to be northern France. This giving of land took place in the 10th century, and Vikings utilized this gifted territory in order to keep hold of their influence in the country.

They were so prominent, in fact, that two Vikings even ascended to the throne of England: Cnut the Great and Sweyn Forkbeard.

When they branched out their conquests into the north Atlantic, the settlement of Iceland quickly became their most important colony. While it is said that Iceland was settled into around the timeframe of 880 A.D., there was no record of the first settlers until 1100 A.D. The Vikings settled, claimed the territory as their own, and promptly began exploring the northern islands and coasts of the North Atlantic. Even though they did raid and pillage cities, they also settled, created wide-ranging colonies, and even traded their own personal goods for others they needed.

But, they did also act as mercenaries.

In the beginning of the culture's journey to quench the thirst of conquest, the Vikings would always return home after their raids. But, once they began to grow in numbers and overtake larger amounts of land, it became a better use of their resources to settle in the lands they conquered instead of leaving to go home and replenish. The expansion of the Viking territory and culture would occur up until the Medieval Warm Period, when the weather anomalies halted their expeditions indefinitely.

Ragnar Lothbrok is a legendary Viking leader who is also a hero within sagas from the Viking age as well as Old Norse poetry. In this literature, Lothbrok ends up distinguishing himself from the crowd of Viking men by initiating and winning multiple raids against England and France during the 9th century. In 1980, it was stated by Hilda Ellis Davidson that many scholars had come to accept part of Lothbrok's story as fact because of the accurate roots that originated his stories, though not all scholars have stepped onto that boat just yet. Scholars like Katherine Holman have pointed out that while Lothbrok's sons are historical figures that lived and died, there is absolutely no evidence of Lothbrok's true-to-life existence. Holman, and many other scholars like her, accept the idea that Lothbrok seems to merely

3

be an amalgam of many different figures in history entwined with literary invention. Ragnar's exact existence is still debated to this day.

However, traditional sources state that Lothbrok was the son of Sigurd Hring, the Swedish king, and a relative of Gudfred, who was the Danish king at the time. He married three times: first, to shield-maiden Lagertha; second, to the noblewoman Thora Brogarhjortr; and third, to the Norse queen Aslaug. He is the father to several historical Vikings such as Sigurd Snake-in-the-Eye, Ivar the Boneless, and Halfdan Ragnarsson. These stories also tell of the fact that Lothbrok was captured by King Aella of Northumbria and would eventually die in a pit of snakes the king threw him into.

There are many significant medieval sources that mention Ragnar Lothbrok. Among these are the Gesta Danorum, which is a 12th-century work by Saxo Grammaticus (a Christian Danish chronicler); the legendary sagas entitled Tale of Ragnar's Sons and Tale of Ragnar Lothbrok; and the Krakumai, which is a 12th-century Scottish skaldic poem said to be Lothbrok's death song.

It is astounding to many people that a man such as Lothbrok could be mentioned and described in as many abstract sources as he is without ever having his history nailed with any accuracy. This prominent figure of legend is mentioned not only in stories and sagas, but texts that modern scholars regard as historical chronicles, and yet there has been little-to-no proof of this Viking's true existence.

Supposedly.

In scholarly sources and stories alike, however, one prevailing fact stands out from all of them: that Ragnar Lothbrok was a Viking warlord who raided England and France. That much is a part of every story ever told about him, so that much has been taken by many as fact. One of the most scholarly of all materials from this timeframe, Anglo-Saxon Chronicles, actually lays out confirmations of the stories surrounding Lothbrok and even provides details of his actions, choices, and deeds that ultimately had a great impact on 9th-century history and how the sons he fathered would end up carrying on his legacy within the Viking culture.

Lothbrok ruled as a king in Denmark for a while, and during this time period him and his sons ruthlessly raided France on multiple occasions. There are some accounts that link Lothbrok to the brutal attack on Paris where 111 Christians were hanged during the pillage.

Lothbrok made his fortune and built his reputation upon raiding powerful kingdoms and lands, and it has been alleged on many occasions that he would attack people while they were praying in church because that is when someone was at their most vulnerable point.

Lothbrok was also a professional at utilizing a sudden charge tactic called a "blitzkrieg" in order to surprise forces who were disciplined and well-organized. Similar to the "guerilla warfare" that the colonies would utilize against the British during the American war for Independence, Lothbrok would have the upper hand by surprising his enemies and stray away from prior memorized organizational tactics. It was a disorienting attack that led him to many victories in kingdoms that were more prominent than the Vikings were during that time period.

France was the main target of his raids for quite some time, and because of this the country suffered greatly. There is actually an account where Lothbrok captured the entire city of Paris and held it for ransom. This forced King Charles to pay 7,000 pounds as the ransom for them letting an entire city go free; this account that solidifies Lothbrok's ruthless tactics in war.

It is well-known that, besides mainland Europe, the Vikings also raided Scotland, Ireland, and England. Many different coastal areas would eventually fall to the Norse invaders, and many at the hands of Lothbrok himself. But, the reason why France was so tasty to the Vikings at the time was because the Frankish royal family was in constant quarrel, and their factions were weakening the country as a whole. The Vikings then looked to exploit this faction and seized the opportunity to settle their first southwest colony in Gascony. It was an area that had essentially been abandoned, and the Vikings took up residence there and flourished.

There were other weak spots the Vikings exploited within this Francia area: incursions along the River Seine ended up causing massive amounts of damage to Rouen and Jumieges. The Vikings would then attack these already-weakened areas and pillage them for the treasures that were stored within their monasteries. They found these to be easy prey because of the monk's lack of defensive capabilities, and this is when Lothbrok developed his war tactic of attacking churches when people were praying.

Under Lothbrok's reign, the Vikings had 120 longships and over 5,000 warriors that would go into battle within him whenever they chose to ravage a particular area.

Lothbrok is a legendary Norse ruler and "hero" who became known as "the scourge of England and France." His ruthless tactics, his warlord mind, and his territorial mindset tailored him to be one of the most prominent and achieved Viking warlords the culture had ever seen. There are many people who struggle to believe he existed simply because the stories surrounding his life are so grand. Because of their grandeur and "shock-and-awe" factor, many assume they are simply fairytales or stories blown drastically out of proportion. However, scholarly sources such as the Anglo-Saxon Chronicles paint a different story than a fabled cultural icon: they paint a picture of a true-to-life ruler who sought to exploit, pillage, and raid his way into his fortune while fathering multiple sons who would then carry on his brutal legacy.

Lothbrok had many views and beliefs that guided him during his reign in the Viking culture, and it is these beliefs and views that would lead him to make many of the decisions he made during his lifetime, aiding his rise to power.

Chapter 2: The Viking's Views & Beliefs

When the Vikings made their way to Britain they already had their own Pagan religion and practices. They worshipped many different gods, and the stories they told about their gods, giants, and monsters are known as the Norse myths. In one particular story, Thor (the god of thunder) attempts to prove his strength to the Giant King by attempting to lift a massive cat. The hilarity of the story comes into play when Thor realizes he can only lift one of the cat's paws, resulting in not only his embarrassment but a lesson that wraps itself around the shame that boastful pride can provide. It is stories like these that Vikings used not only as ravenous table-talk during parties, but were also used to teach their children different lessons and values they felt were important.

Odin was the ruler of the Gods as well as the god of magic, poetry, and war. His wife was Frig, and their son was Balder, who was incredibly kind and gentle. Freyja was the goddess of love and fertility, and she has been said to have wept golden tears whenever she was unhappy. She had a twin brother Freyr, and the sacred animal attached to them was the boar. Thor ruled the skies, storms, and thunder, and he had iron gloves, a magic belt, and a hammer. People enjoyed Thor, but did not trust the mysterious trickster god, Loki, and Loki became even more hated when he caused the death of Balder by one of his tricks.

This is where the ideals and traditions of Viking burials comes into play. In the Viking culture, an individual's body was either buried or cremated along with some of their belongings so they could take them into the next world. Viking chiefs were given ship-burials, where their body was loaded onto a boat with their treasures, weapons, and favorite animals. Then, the ship was set on fire and hoisted out to sea while a meditative ceremony and glorious celebration took place as people watched from the shoreline.

It is a big belief the Vikings held that a warrior who was killed in battle was sent to Valhalla, which is a great hall where dead heroes feasted lavishly at massively long tables for the rest of their afterlife. Stories told within the Viking culture state that Odin would send his warrior maidens, called the Valkyries, to ride through the skies in order to bring the dead warriors to Valhalla. These stories also told of how people lived in Midgard, or Middle Earth, and these stories also held entities such as dwarves, giants, and elves. It was stated that the gods and goddesses lived in the sky in a place called Asgard, and that Midgard and Asgard were linked together with a rainbow bridge.

The Vikings also had many tales of monsters, including trolls, sea serpents, dragons, and the fierce wolf Fenrir. This is a particular monster that the gods of Asgard attempted to keep chained up because of its ferocity and ambitious need to slaughter. Animals also played a massive part in the Vikings belief system and the setting of their values because not only were animals attributed to specific gods and goddesses to represent them on Earth, powerful gods like Odin also rode them as a symbol of their power. For example, Odin rode a magical horse named Sleipnir, who had eight legs, which was indicative of not only Odin's position, but of his power and grace. Animals not only dictated power and status, they also dictated perseverance and reverence among the Viking culture.

There is not too much that is known about how the Vikings would actually worship their old gods, all that is known is that they were thought to have had 'magic trees' and wooden temples. It is also speculative that some Vikings may have actually killed captives they took in their pillages and raids and utilized them as human sacrifices. However, these old customs died out after the bulk of the Vikings became Christians. When they landed in Britain, they realized that people had been Christians long before the Vikings actually settled there in the 900s. The British religious influence of Christianity would soon move most Vikings to become Christians, and there are many Viking leaders who would actually go on to establish churches and erect painted stone crosses. Of course, some Vikings would continue to follow their old religion at the same time, but eventually the bulk of them came to lead Christian-based lives that would permeate their culture for many generations after.

The truth of the matter is that there is very little we truly understand about the Viking beliefs, rituals, and other activities pertaining to the gods they worshipped. The most comprehensive form of information we have on the Vikings comes from the Codex Regius which, when translated, literally means 'King's Book.' There is other documentation that was not written until the Vikings and the Scandinavian people had converted to Christianity, but additional information also does come from the Poetic Edda that is contained within the Codex Regius. This Edda is a collection of Old Norse poems and stories that cover many different mythological tales and practices that were utilized in the Norse traditions, and it is from these ancient documents that we have references to many pagan acts they enacted when they worshipped specific gods and deities.

One of the greatest beliefs we know to be fully fleshed-out are the universal realms the Vikings believed existed. These realms were a way the Vikings theorized and explained the expanse of the universe around them, which meant that, even back during the 1000s, space exploration was on the minds of people standing on this very planet. The Vikings looked to the sky and found ways to reconcile what they saw and were oddly settled by the fact that they were not the only ones that existed within the expansive universe they understood to exist.

In the universe as they explained it, there are nine different realms that house a multitude of homes, or planets. These realms are populated by humans, gods, sinners, and giants. It is these realms that are bonded by the Viking world tree, known as Yggdrasil, and this tree houses special powers. Its home is rooted in the very center of the universe, and the three primary realms were Niflheim, Asgard, and Midgard. But, there are many others the Vikings believed existed.

Niflheim was the world of mist, and literally translates to 'land of freezing mist.' It is dark, cold, and clouded within this mist, and this particular realm is unfriendly to say the least. Neflheim is the realm that is located to the far north and was housed on the lowest rung of the outlined Norse universe. This is the area that was reserved for people who broke Viking oaths, criminals who did what they did for no good reason, and cold-blooded murderers.

Midgard was the middle realm, which is the land of the mortals in ancient Norse times. This is where Earth existed, and this is a human area that was linked to the home of the gods (Asgard) by the Rainbow Bridge. Midgard hung on one of the middle rungs in the middle realm of the Norse universe, and was the closest connected realm to Asgard, despite the power difference. This idea sheds light on how the Vikings ranked themselves among god-like figures, giving off the idea that they were the closest to their gods and goddesses that they worshipped because they were the most powerful mortals to exist and could easily be like them. This type of relationship between the realm they existed on and the realm the gods existed on sheds light on the inherent pride the Viking culture sustained within their values.

Asgard was the home of the Aesir gods, which was led by Odin. Asgard in and of itself was home to many different realms inside of its boundaries, including Valhalla. So, the Vikings belief in Valhalla actually took them to Asgard in the afterlife if they were to die a heroic death in the middle of war. Asgard was centrally located in the middle of the Viking world as they theorized it, and it was on the highest rung of the Norse universe. This area was specifically populated by elite gods, including Frig, Thor, and Loki.

Vanahemir was home of the Vanir, a group of Norse gods that included Freyja, Freyr, and their father Njord. These were the gods that were known for their different associations with love, beauty, virility, and passion. This was another realm inhabited by elite gods, but the gods of Vanir were later joined with the Aesir gods to become members of that primary group housed in Asgard. The only difference between the gods and Vanahemir and the gods and Asgard was that the gods and Vanahemir were symbols and rulers of everything having to do with romance, seduction, lust, sex, and fertility.

Jotunheim was the land of the mighty Norse giants, who were a menacing group and troubling to both humans and gods that lived within all of the Viking realms. Jotunheim housed hugely proportionate creatures that were considered massive forces of nature by the old Norse myths. Some of them are depicted as massive blue giants, some of them are depicted as massive tree giants, and some of them are depicted by massive fire giants, but the main thing that links all of them is that these massive creatures and monsters were forces of nature to be reckoned with that even the powerful gods of Asgard and Vanahemir shook at the mere mention of.

Alfheim was the land of the elves within this Norse universe, and this is the particular realm that was home to one of two specific groups of elves: the first being the light elves. They were a race that the Norse reported to be very pleasing to the eye, but that is all the information we really have on this race of elves. The other race was the dark elves; whose home was in Svartalfheim.

Svartalfeim was known within these Norse tales to be home of the dark elves, which were often referred to as swart elves. There is a very interesting point of uncertainty with this realm because many sources we have that break down the outlining of the Viking universe lists this realm as home of the dwarves as well. However, many people do not know whether the dark elves were also dwarfs or if the dark elves were just not as important as the light elves, so they were lumped with another group that was not as important to the Vikings as others. The reason why is because light elves and their pleasant demeanor and physical beauty are talked about much more in the Norse tales and myths than the dark elves.

Muspelheim was the realm of fire as was ruled by the giant Surtr. Surtr was the leader of the fire giants that inhabited Muspelheim and became incredibly famous for his sword that burned brighter than any other sword created in all of the nine realms. Within Norse mythology, it is said that Muspelheim and Niflheim eventually met, and this is when fire and ice joined to create water. This means that not only did the Vikings believe in these realms that separated the universe into different sectors, they also believed that many of the elements bestowed upon them to help them live were also rooted in the creation, and interaction, between the realms of the universe.

Helheim is the last of the nine realms, and it was known as the underworld of Norse mythology. This was home to the being who oversaw this realm, called Hel. Hel was the daughter of Loki, and her realm of Helheim was actually situated within the bowels of Neflheim. Helheim was the place Vikings would go if they died from natural causes (or simply not in battle) and it was impossible to leave once you arrived. Helheim was surrounded by the river Gjoll and was guarded by a devilish giant hound that was known as Garm, and this was a place that was feared by many Vikings. It is this fear of Helheim and its monotonous existence that lit a fire underneath many generations of Vikings to ravage, pillage, and plunder many cities in order to overtake them: because dying in battle would lead them to a glorious place, while dying any other way lead them to a place of unworthiness.

It is assumed that Ragnar Lothbrok held many of the same beliefs, especially given the fact that he was seen as a warlord figurehead within the Viking community. It is theorized that in order to rise to that prominent of a position, an individual not only has to have a deep passion for the culture's belief system, but that individual also has to uphold those belief systems and customs to their highest regard. This is why Lothbrok was the fearless raider he was: because not only did he want all of his soldiers eventually ending up in the halls of Valhalla, but he also wanted the families back in their homelands that they all held in high esteem to be taken care of.

And Ragnar, just like many other Vikings, had a sprawling family whom he cared for deeply.

Chapter 3: Ragnar's Family

Depending on which documents you read, there are different layouts of Ragnar's family. However, some facts are undisputed: Lothbrok took on multiple wives, had many sons, and had twice as many grandsons before he died. Popular theories state that Lothbrok had three wives: Lagertha (who was a shield-maiden), Aslaug (who was a warrior queen), and Thora Town-Hart (who was a noblewoman). However, there are some accounts that do mention a fourth wife.

Nevertheless, one of the undisputed facts is that these women bore him many sons. Two of the most popular sons were Bjorn Ironside and Ivar The Boneless, though some other individuals may have heard of Ubba, Hvitserk, and Halfdan Ragnarsson. Even though it has yet to be proven that Lothbrok was, in fact, an actual person, it has been proven that many of his infamous sons did, in fact, live and thrive during these times.

Lothbrok also had several daughters among those sons, but there is no accurate information we have today in regards to their names. We know Lagertha gave him two of them, and we see the names Ragnhild Ragnarsdottir and Åløf Ragnarsdóttir appear alongside hers, which leads many Viking scholars to draw the assumption that these are two of his daughters' names.

Here is how Ragnar's family tree goes when you combine all saga accounts of his family:

- He was the son of Sigurd, King of Fofnersbane, and Ingild Gandolfsdottir

- He had brothers and sisters, as well as a half sister (Hring Sigurdsdatter)

- Other siblings were Gorm, Sigurd, Geva, Bjorn, and Miss.

- Husband of Aslaug

- Father of Ivar "The Boneless" Ragnarsson, Sigurd "Snake-In-The-Eye" Ragnarsson, and Ubbe Ragnarsson.

- Husband of Lagertha

- Father of Fridleiv Ragnarsson, Ragnhild Ragnarsdottir, and Åløf Ragnarsdóttir.

- Husband of Thora

- Father of Bjorn "Ironside" Jarnsida, Rathbarth Ragnarsson, and Dunyat Ragnarrson.

- Husband of Svanloga

In the ninth book of the Gesta Danorum, Lothbrok is genuinely listed as the grandson of the King of Norway, Siward, which would make sense seeing as King Siward is said to have produced a son whom he named "Sigurd," which is said to be Lothbrok's father. Though, there are some accounts that paint Lothbrok as a farmer who rose up the ranks of the Vikings in order to become as powerful as he was. But, the widely accepted notion is that Lothbrok was of royal blood.

However, Lothbrok's name was not always as such. His wife, Lagertha, was a woman placed into a brothel by someone within his kingdom. When he came across Lagertha in the brothel he was so beyond impressed with her fighting skills and skills as a warrior that he pursued her relentlessly in an attempt to woo her affections. However, Lagertha was determined to completely disregard his advances, and even took steps to protect herself from him by placing a bear and a hound outside her place of residence in order to guard her front door.

But, Ragnar came along and slayed the beasts she placed within his path, and she had no choice but to accept his hand in marriage. While it did not last forever, it did last long enough for her to bear their son and two daughters. What ruined their marriage, however, was Lothbrok's anger. He became angry as to the fact that Lagertha worked so hard to repel his advances, and he ended up divorcing her over it. Soon after that, he began pursuing Thora.

Thora, by the way, was the daughter of King Herodd, who was the king of the Swedes. And, in pursuing her as well, he had to fight and kill wild beasts in order to win over her affections. It was found that Thora had raised two deadly serpents that became enormous in size as they grew. Thora's father promised Lothbrok his daughter's hand if he could kill those snakes so he could be rid of them forever. At first, this was a challenge set forth to all the men in the village, and many died attempting to kill these snakes. Lothbrok was the only one truly successful at the endeavor, and that is because he studied what the other men who had come before him had done wrong.

Lothbrok and Aslaug's story is told in the Tale of Ragnar Ladbrok. Within this story, Aslaug is the daughter of Sigurd and Brynhildr, and she is the wife that not only bore him the most sons (four, to be exact), but she is also the wife that outlived Lothbrok. Apparently, she was so concerned about Lothbrok returning to England that she ended up trying to get word to him to warn him against traveling. Lothbrok, of course, would not heed her warnings, so Aslaug imbued upon him a magical shirt. And, for a while, the shirt worked until it was ordered to be taken from him, and the removal of this shirt is what would ultimately lead Lothbrok to his death.

The Anglo Saxon Chronicle also has mentions of Lothbrok's family. It is a collection of seven distinct manuscripts that are written in relation to England's own history and historical texts. According to our own modern-day encyclopedias, the Anglo Saxon Chronicle is one of the primary sources of England's early history.

So, many scholars take what is within the walls of this text as basic historical fact.

This is why many scholars believe Ragnar Lothbrok was an actual person: because he is mentioned several times within these chronicles, especially in regards to his family. Ivar The Boneless, Ubbe, and Halfdan are all mentioned in this text.

Specifically, it talks about Lothbrok's sons' 865 East Anglia invasion. Historically, these three sons got together to form the Great Heathen Army in direct retaliation to their father's murder at the hands of King Aelle, and even more scholars believe that this retaliation truly did take place because it is one of the only moments mentioned in all three sources recounting Lothbrok's life.

However, the accounts leading up to this formation are different depending on the saga or story you read. In one saga, it is said that when his sons heard of how their father was murdered, they all reacted with sorrow in their own way. It is told that Hvitserk was playing a game and gripped a game piece so hard he ended up bleeding from his fingernails digging into his skin. Bjorn Ironside is said to have grabbed a spear he was practicing with so tightly he ended up leaving impressions upon its staff, and it is said that Sigurd Snake-Eye was trimming his nails and cut himself all the way down to the bone and almost lost his finger because of it.

It is stated that Ivar the Boneless is the one that swore vengeance for his father's death. This was a time-honored Viking tradition, where if someone from the community was slayed in a violent and unnecessary way (that is not on the battlefield) that the village would come for the life of the one who ripped it away. So, the Great Heathen Army was put together with Lothbrok's sons at the helm, and they met their father's murderer in battle and captured him. Ivar the Boneless, in this story, got his vengeance by committing King Aelle to an exceedingly painful death.

Ivar the Boneless is, by far, the most infamous of Ragnar's sons. He was a berserker warrior that was feared for his ruthless and brutal tactics in any sort of fighting scenario he found himself in. He was cruel, violent, and a volatile warlord that served as a warrior in Denmark where he became the head of an entire army made up of berserker warriors. Ivar is also said to have been more like a giant than an ordinary man, so we can gather the impression that he was exceedingly tall for the average Viking male.

Many people have wondered, however, where Ivar's nickname "The Boneless" came from, and after reading multiple accounts of his life and analyzing the few drawings and renderings we have of him, it has been theorized that Ivar dealt with a medical issue called benign hypermobility syndrome. This essentially results in an individual's joints being very flexible and loose, and it is coupled with a degenerative bone issue that would have resulted in his lower body being much weaker than the rest of his body.

In many accounts, it is stated that Ivar was carried into battle on a giant shield by the men he commanded, and it is this shield that turned him into a deadly killing mechanism. Because his lower body was theorized to be incredibly weak, the theory stands that this would have prompted Ivar to over-train his upper body in order to compensate and not be weak in the eyes of his community. The stories and sagas also tell us that he was lethally accurate when he utilized a longbow, and they praised his warrior attitude and lifestyle despite the medical condition surrounding his legs.

Ivar was not simply cruel, however, but also incredible cunning. He was sly on the battlefield as well as brutal, and it made him a well-rounded warrior that was praised within his community. He is single-handedly responsible for the 865 invasion of England, and ended up launching the largest British Isles invasion in England's recorded history. Under Ivar's command, the Viking forces and warriors had absolutely no opposition. If they landed in a city and began to raid and pillage, many of the locals would raise the money in order to bribe the Vikings to stay away.

And every time Ivar was offered money, he would take it... but that did not mean he would not continue pillaging their villages and homes.

He held one of the largest command of Viking warriors under his hand when he was at the helm, and this unified command under Ivar The Boneless was one of the first in Viking and English history. Ivar's overall plan was to pick off, one by one, all of the Anglo-Saxon kingdoms so the Vikings could settle and rule East Anglia. The Vikings stripped the countryside of their food and resources, and left it in ruins whenever they would move on to their next target.

While it seems horrendous and jaw-dropping to us, Ivar would have been considered the model son in Lothbrok's eyes and time. Taking after his father in war and subsequently outdoing him would have been the pride that caused Lothbrok's chest to swell, and ironically enough it is Lothbrok's death that arose this cruel and brutal lifestyle from the depths of Ivar's soul.

However, just because his son outdid him within the world of war and pillaging does not mean that Ragnar was not an expert when it came to those same war tactics. Many outlandish and grand stories are told of Lothbrok's war-based encounters, and they were talked about at victory parties for decades to come within the Viking community.

Chapter 4: The Mighty Ragnar At War

"Lothbrok" was not always Ragnar's surname. When Lothbrok wedded Aslaug, she made him a pair of britches from animal hides and skins in order to keep his legs from becoming wartorn and to aid in his warmth during his travels. "Lothbrok" literally means "Hairy Britches," coming from the literal animal hairs he wore as pants as gifts from his wife. Ragnar was a very boastful man, claiming he was a direct descendent of the great Odin and preaching that this was where he obtained his war tactics from. Many of the tales surrounding Ragnar Lothbrok originate in the sagas and stories told about him, and some scholars and historians believe that if Ragnar was a real man, his stories have been so overtold and overblown because of his incredible feats that this is how they have taken on their God-like essence.

Tradition states that after Ragnar's birth mother, Alfild, passed away, his father sought out the love and company of a beautiful princess names Alfsol, Princess of Jutland. He took her as his wife when Ragnar was still but a boy, but it states that Alfol's family was not happy that she married Sigurd. So, Sigurd challenged her entire family and defeated them single-handedly in a battle. But, Alfsol's father could not accept this treason, and proclaimed that he would rather lose his daughter to the halls of Valhalla than to Sigurd, so Alfsol's father gave her a cup of poison to drink. Sigurd was so distraught over losing Alfsol that he arranged for her body to be placed upon a funeral pyre upon his finest ship. Then, when the fires shot from the skies had set the ship ablaze and the ship was cut from its directive moorings, Ragnar's father ended up springing aboard the ship, stabbing himself in the stomach, and was consumed alongside the body of his dead beloved as their fiery ship sailed out to sea.

This had a profound impact on young Ragnar. He felt abandoned by a father who chose a woman who was not even his mother over staying with him, and he felt that if he had been a better son... a stronger son... than his father would have stayed. This is the background behind how Ragnar trained. This was how Lothbrok's mind worked: in all of the raids, wars, and pillaging he did there was simply a young boy starving for his father to choose him over her.

Him over love.

And it is because of what his father did and how it juxtaposed the wrathful strength of a Viking man that caused Ragnar to study war tactics. Whether his proclamation of being Odin's son was to bolster his own ruthless warrior reputation or whether it was a psychological attempt to replace the father he felt was weak and absent, none of us will ever know. There is a certain psychological twinge to it that has the potential to fuel great fires throughout young Ragnar's life, but the truth of the matter is the tales that surround his life, whether it be war stories or familial stories, all now look a little different after understanding that a young boy had lost his mother and then been abandoned by his lovesick father.

There is a running theory that people who were heroes and demigods as we see them today were nothing more than common human beings who did extraordinary things. Thus, their extraordinary things were rewarded with stories about them being told to later generations. This idea of storytelling, though once began as a noble way to honor the dead and fallen, was passed on as an art form and gathered steam as a form of entertainment to raise children with specific morals and values in order to further the cultivation of society. The bombastic nature of these stories as told over time is what give them their godlike nature.

Many scholars who believe Ragnar truly did exist believe that this is the phenomenon that took over his life stories.

Lothbrok was believed to be "the scourge of France and England," meaning he was a disease upon which all land fell to dust whenever he would step his foot onto dry land. That is a powerful metaphor for just one man, but his war stories are very grand, to say the least. Lothbrok happily raided Northumbria, which were Anglican kingdoms, and Wessex on several occasions. He also took on the Kingdom of West Francia, which sealed itself off with the siege of Paris that befell in 845.

In 793, the Vikings (led by Lothbrok himself) attacked a Christian monastery known as Lindisfarne off the coast of England. They pillaged, raided, destroyed, and leveled the entire monastery before making off with every single piece of treasure their longships could hold. This was the attack that would strike fear into the hearts of many across Europe, and it is the raid that put Lothbrok on the map, so to speak.

This was also the date historians would recognize as the beginning of the brutal Viking history and their particular role in it. This is the official beginning of the "Viking Era" and the first of multiple raids Ragnar Lothbrok would wreak upon that land, who became a very quick enemy to the religion of Christianity. In fact, Ragnar was so ruthless and cared so little for religion that he would attack Christians during their in-church celebrations because he knew that is when they would be most vulnerable. He would utilize this tactic to catch multiple individuals off-guard, and he would slaughter them in droves, even as they were kneeling in churches.

Lothbrok would frequently lead pirate raids into France by utilizing the river system to sail his longships and his fleets into the heart of the Frankish empire, and this is the tactic that was used for the infamous raid in 845 that we previously mentioned. He ended up commanding over five thousand Viking berserkers and warriors in one fleet comprised over 120 longships. He was going to utilize his strategy of attacking on a holy day so the city would already be at its knees (Easter, to be exact), but news of their coming had already been figured out and dispersed to the French army. So, by the time they had gotten there most of the population of Paris had already fled. The Vikings flooded in anyway and spread throughout the homes and businesses, plundering and taking what was not theirs, and ended up gaining the greatest loot any of their historical raids had produced.

During this raid, the French king, Charles the Bald (who was the grandson of Charlemagne) not only ordered the clearing out of the population but also ordered some troops to stay behind and fend off the Lothbrok's advances. However, the Vikings easily defeated the first divisional wall of Frenchmen and the rest retreated in terror. Then, after they took their historical plunder of things that were not theirs, the Vikings withdrew after taking one last thing from the Frenchmen.

7,000 pounds.

When the Vikings entered into Paris, they took the French king hostage and forced those that had cleared out to pay for their breathing king's head. They occupied the city while the townspeople raised the money, and when it was finally raised and given over to the Vikings, they released King Charles the Bald to his people and left.

There are some accounts that state that the King himself paid the ransom with 7,000 pounds of silver and forced them out, where they then returned to their homeland to celebrate the spoils they had brought back. Nevertheless, no matter how it happened, what we do know was that besides pillaging an entire city, they also took a significant amount of bribed money along with them just so they would leave without doing any more harm than they had already done.

Lothbrok continued his raids throughout France for the bulk of the 9th century and is even noted for his great participation in many of Denmark's early civil wars.

The truth of the matter is that the Vikings were not the first to raid these areas. We do know that they started their raiding and pillaging in Scotland and other areas of England well before Lothbrok came to be. The first account in any story or saga comes from as early as the late 700s. However, Ragnar's stories stick with people because he was the first to begin attempting to colonize those areas the Vikings pillaged and conquered. Ragnar did not just have a thirst for bounty and treasure, he had a thirst for expanding their culture and kingdom into areas of prominence.

Many could even say this was a way to outdo his father, to show that he would never abandon his family, his sons, or his people the way his father did.

And he succeeded, in some regard. By 911, Rouen (the capital of Normandy) was controlled by Vikings who ended up pledging their allegiance to the French crown, ironically enough. The Normans who are known for conquering England in 1066 were largely of Viking origin who had pledged their lives and fates to France and the King who was in control at the time.

Ragnar Lothbrok was a powerful warrior, an abandoned son, and a ruthless pillager. He led many successful raids and was the powerhouse engine behind many successful battles in Denmark's multiple civil wars. He led his community with power, strength, and authority, and there are some people that theorize that his taking on of multiple wives was a way to show his father, who abandoned him at such a young age, that a man could love, lose, and still be there for his family.

In many ways, it is possible to see the psychology of an angry, wounded, abandoned little boy in every single action Ragnar Lothbrok ever took.

His stories are grand and his tactics were ruthless. He attacked when he knew people would be weakened and had absolutely no regard for other cultures. His want and desire to further the Viking race and culture meant obliterating other people who walked into his path, and he asserted that aggressiveness every chance he obtained. He was feared by many and respected by many more in his culture, and his sons and daughters had a great deal of reverence towards their father and all he had accomplished.

His raids throughout Europe are accounted for in many historical documents. While some details shift with each story, the overarching basis for the "story" is always the same in every single account. We do know that a raid took place in Paris in 845 around the time of Easter, and we do know that the city was left to ruin even after the Vikings were paid 7,000 pounds to let the King go that they took hostage. We do know that a monastery was raided in 793 and that it was left in utter ruin after being taken for everything it had to provide. These facts, to all historians, are indisputable because they are found in the same order and described in much the same way each time.

However, the power of his stories and his prominence in the community can be seen in the reaction of his sons to the death of their father. We already know that Lothbrok married many times and fathered many different sons and daughters with his wives, and we even know about the Great Heathen Army that was formed at the hands of his sons who were irate at the murder of their father.

What we have not discussed yet, however, were the circumstances surrounding Ragnar Lothbrok's death.

Chapter 5: Ragnar's Death

Ragnar Lothbrok's death, just like his war stories, has many facets, tales, and conjurings. The most popular tale tells not only the story of Lothbrok's death, but of how his son's reacted to the news of his death.

There are two main stories of his death: one is the fact that Lothbrok had contracted wounds in his infamous Paris siege, and from those wounds and his time in France he contracted diarrhea. Several descriptions of this cause of death lead historians to believe that if this is the account of Lothbrok's death, then it was something similar to dysentery. However, the second story that is told in the Anglo-Saxon Chronicle tells that Lothbrok met his ultimate demise in battle at the hands of his enemies.

In this particular account of his death, Lothbrok and his armies were on their way back home from the Paris siege and their ship ended up washing ashore on what is now understood as the coast of the Northumbria Kingdom. When they washed ashore, their ship was attacked and Lothbrok himself was held for ransom numerous times, just like he had held King Charles the Bald ransom in the middle of his Paris siege.

King Aella of Northumbria had sworn vengeance on Ragnar Lothbrok for quite some time, so he decided to take his revenge after pillaging the infamous pillagers and holding him for multiple ransoms that the Vikings were more than willing to pay. He took Ragnar and threw him into a deep, dark pit of snakes, and left him to a painful and gruesome death at the hand of the man that wanted to kill him the most.

During his time in the snake pit, it is said that he sang a particular Norse hymn that promised the King his sons would retaliate and avenge him. Remember how we mentioned earlier that these tales do not only talk of Ragnar's death, but of his son's reactions?

That is exactly what happened.

After learning of their father's death, Ivar The Boneless swore vengeance upon King Aella, and formed what we have already talked about as the Great Heathen Army. This army was formed and, in 866, sailed with the strict purpose of avenging Lothbrok's death.

And they were successful in their raid.

When his sons sailed the seas and landed in the Kingdom of Northumbria, they captured not only the king responsible for the killing, which was King Aella, but also the king of East Anglia that stood by and allowed it to happen, which was King Edmund. They first captured King Edmund, bound him to a tree, and Ivar The Boneless earned his ruthless title by shooting him with arrows until he died, before beheading him just to make sure he could never recuperate.

The Great Heathen Army then went on to sack the city of York and ultimately found King Aella in battle, who they defeated and captured. They took Aella into the middle of the sacked city after everyone had fallen and had either been captured, killed, or ordered to retreat, and they subjected the king to one of the most bloodied and painful traditions of killing the Vikings had in their arsenal: the blood eagle.

This method had several distinct stages that inflicted multiple points of pain, open wounds, and humiliation before the individual ultimately suffered an untimely death. First, the victim would be wholly restrained and faced down. Then, the rough shape of an eagle with its wings outstretched would be carved into the skin of his back while the individual was pressed into the ground. This would not only be painful, but would cause the individual to inhale whatever dirt or loose particles they were being pressed into. It was not uncommon for people to choke and suffocate at this stage.

Then, the individual's ribs would be hacked away from his spine with an ax and the skin on both sides would be pulled out towards the person inflicting the torture in order to resemble the pair of "wings" of the eagle carved into the individual's back. Then, if the victim was still alive at this point, they would rub salt into the vast wounds.

26

Then, as if that was not enough, the exposed lungs of the unfortunate individual would be ripped from their body and laid over their "wings," which would offer those watching this taking place the sight of a final bird-esque "fluttering" of his lungs as they watch the individual slowly die.

Yikes.

Most people usually died of a heart attack because of the great deal of pain, but some unfortunate souls would stay alive long enough to bleed to death through their wounds.

There are a couple of accounts, including the account in the Anglo-Saxon Chronicle, that states that both of the kings were slain in the battle that took place in York, but many other accounts not only describe what a "bloody eagle" is, but state that the most popular individual to sustain it was King Aella.

However gruesome the story surrounding Lothbrok's death and its effects that rang throughout the nations, Ragnar's legacy continued for generations through his descendants. His legacy and his name made an impact on the structure of every single region the Vikings laid waste to and claimed from the moment of his death up until present times. Two centuries after his death, the descendants of Ragnar Lothbrok and his sons ended up settling on the west coast of France, naming it "the Land of Northmen."

Today, this is what we call modern-day "Normandy."

Ragnar was a powerful ruler and eventual Lord under the Danish King Horik II. There is one account that states that Rangar not only survived the siege of Paris, but also the snake pit in order to make it back home. This particular saga states that he passed away in Denmark simply because of old age, and that is probably why this particular story, if true, was buried.

If Lothbrok died of old age instead of in battle, no matter how ruthless or long-lasting his raids and his legacy was, he would not have entered Valhalla to feast with the Vikings he led into battle. To the Viking culture, this would have brought great shame to his family, so if this story is true it is understandable why the Vikings and his descendants would have wanted to cover it up with other stories told.

However, many historians do not believe this is the true story because it is only accounted for in one saga, and this particular saga is not taken as historical fact, but only seen as a mere tool to entertain children of the Viking era.

Outside of that one saga, all sources are in agreement that Ragnar Lothbrok died in England, it is simply the matter in which he died that is up for debate within these stories and sources. Some versions preach that he was killed by King Aella in the snake pit, and some sources state he was murdered in East Anglia after befriending the traitorous King Edmund. If King Edmund was, in fact, traitorous to the Vikings and to Lothbrok, that could give another reason as to why his sons went after him with their Great Heathen Army in order to kill him in the fashion that Ivar The Boneless did.

Another thing that has to be understood about the Great Heathen Army and their raid on England was the fact that it sparked a 14-year long war against all of the Saxon Kingdoms. Within this war, Ivar The Boneless rose to his status of a berserker warrior who was ruthless and cruel, but he was not above being paid off in order to attack one group over another.

After all, the Vikings were not just senseless killers, they also wanted all of your precious treasures, too.

There is a brief story that is accounted for that states that Ragnar's sons, who led the Great Heathen Army throughout this war, were given many horses by the new King of East Anglia that rose to power after they executed King Edmund in order to stay away from their particular slice of the kingdom and attack other kingdoms around them. This was a strategy utilized by the new King of East Anglia in order to expand into and settle onto the surrounding lands he had wished for but had no way to acquire.

Like many of the incredible heroes that dictate the overall story of basic human history, Ragnar Lothbrok is a larger-than-life figure whose story and supposed existence holds immense historical and cultural significance. In many ways, he is a metaphorical and physical representation of the entity of the Viking culture. He represents a relict of a dead age who is just as complex as he as contradictory. However, regardless of whatever direction you choose to take Ragnar Lothbrok's story based on the stories, sagas, and historical accounts of him, it is very safe to say that understanding his beguiling nature and history will not only take you a lifetime, but be incredibly intriguing in the process in terms of how Ragnar's life, experiences, and tales intersect to create the "man" he is considered in history.

One of the main problems for historians that disables them from stating Ragnar Lothbrok was a true-to-life Viking that truly lived is the fact that his dates are hard to nail down. Because they do not have accurate dates to work with, many of the dates scholars have settled on do not fit up with the timeline that is laid out in historical books we do currently recognize as fact.

For example, it states in the Passio Sancti Eadmundi that King Edmund the Martyr (the one that died at the hands of Ivar The Boneless) actually died tied to a tree and shot to death with arrows in 869, which means the tale of the Great Heathen Army sailing to do this exact thing could not have occurred in 866. It also states in this same historical book that King Aella of Northumbria met his fate at the hands of the Vikings with the "blood eagle" in 867, meaning his death did not occur right after King Edmund's, nor did it occur in the year many scholars preach who do believe Ragnar was a real human being.

However, even though the dates are subject to debate among scholars and historians alike, what is not argued is the fact that King Edmund and King Aella did suffer their fate at the hands of Ivar The Boneless, whom every scholar and historian has declared did exist. It is through the deaths of these two kings that Ivar The Boneless earned the reputation for the most feared Viking of his time period, and it is what would help him rise to the type of distinction his father, Ragnar Lothbrok, had within his community.

Even though historians and scholars can prove, without a doubt, that many of Ragnar's ruthless sons did live and thrive during the Viking era, it still remains to be confirmed that Ragnar

Lothbrok himself was a Viking man that lived and died just as his sons did.

So, why?

Why do scholars and historians have such a hard time nailing down whether Ragnar Lothbrok ever existed?

Well, besides the debacle of dates that do not line up, there are other reasons historians theorize.

Chapter 6: Why Historians Debate Ragnar's Existence

Ragnar Lothbrok's existence is one of the most debated things in history. One of the things that makes it difficult to figure out whether he lived are the conflicting dates, but the other is a bit more philosophical than that.

When historians and scholars debate Lothbrok's existence, they ask whether he was "historical," and that word needs to be defined more clearly. Do they mean that what is said about him is historically accurate? Do they simply mean that he was a part of history? On the former end, some of the sieges that are contributed to Lothbrok did take place, but that does not mean that end can claim victory. On the latter end, a Viking name entitled "Reginheri" appears many times in the Frankish annals, specifically around the same times as Ragnar Lothbrok's raids, but just because that is written down in texts we deem "historical" does not mean the latter can claim victory either.

Neither of the two extremes are truly acceptable within a serious debate and talk on the subject, so it only stands to reason that the combination of the two, the "middle ground", is what people are ultimately looking for. So, for the purposes of this chapter, "historical" means both a documented person and the fact that Ragnar performed a many number of actions and deeds that were, in fact, as legendary as his stories.

And, those stories have to somewhat coincide in their basic truths.

While the burden of proof falls onto the shoulders of those who claim Ragnar Lothbrok was a true-to-life, historical individual, historians and scholars have failed, time and time again, to come up with enough proof that falls under this "middle ground" criterion to truly be able to declare themselves victorious within the argument itself. But, this "Reginheri" figure does deserve a second look.

Records claim Ragnar Lothbrok was a 9th-century Viking, but the closest name to "Ragnar" that we have recorded down that lived during this time is a Viking named "Reginheri," which is the Latin equivalent to the name "Ragnar." According to the Frankish annals, Reginheri died in 845 as stated in the Annales Bertiniani (the Annals of St. Bertin). Many people have taken to Reginheri and interpreted this Viking as an historical prototype of sorts for the actual Ragnar Lothbrok. But, the issue stands that since Reginheri died in 845 in France, he could not have physically participated in the events that are so well-attributed to Lothbrok himself.

And that throws a massive kink in the theory that Reginheri and Ragnar are, in fact, the same person, if you choose to believe the sagas and stories talked about within this text.

In addition to that blatant issue, there is also no evidence with the Frankish annals that Reginheri was the father of anyone, much less the sons that came to conquer and slay two of the most prominent kings in the Saxon empires. So, even though the name is accurate, the Viking Reginheri that did exist fails to quality himself with the criterion mentioned above. And with that declaration, there are no other Norsemen named "Ragar" during that suggested time period that could have possibly been known for these feats.

Well, what about "Lothbrok"? Maybe there is no "Ragnar" that fits the time period, but maybe there is a "Lothbrok." Unfortunately, no record gives this name either as historically significant. But, it does make an actual appearance 200 years after Ragnar's supposed untimely death. The name actually appears as "Lothbroc" in the Gesta Normannorum Ducum, written by William of Jumieges in 1070. In this text, it states that "Lothbroc" was the father of Bjorn Ironside.

Now, there is a Viking named Bjorn that is verified wholly and completely by contemporary chronicles, but does not have the nickname of "Ironside." However, when Adam of Brenmen picked up writing this text soon after Jumieges demise, he wrote that Ivar was the son of "Lodparchus." Even though Ragnar is not apparent or written about in any of the sources we deem contemporary and historical that mention his sons' names, there is another potential issue:

"Lothbroka" is the only other closest rendition of "Lothbrok" we do have in these contemporary writings, and by all accounts of language derivatives, "Lothbroka" is the female derivative of "Lothbrok."

"Lothbrok" is never a name out rightly mentioned, but "Lothbroka" is.

There is another way historians have looked at this issue, and that is by searching for names inquiring about a "Ragnall." In the Fragmentary Annals of Ireland, there is an item of interest that has been pointed out quite a bit as a possible source of the legend related to Ragnar Lothbrok. Within this text, formerly known as the "Three Fragments," Ragnall (Rognvald), who is the son of Alpdan (Halfdan, the king of Norway), is mentioned. Alongside that tidbit of information that has been exposed, his exploits prior to the infamous fall of the Danes and York are also given in strict context and with enough detail that many historians, agreeable or not, have given rise to the idea that Ragnall could in fact be our legendary Ragnar Lothbrok.

But, even with that criteria fitting, there are still massive issues with this particular interpretation. First, Ragnall and Ragnar are nowhere close to the same name, even though they are familiar in spelling. It would be the equivalent of telling someone "Daniel" and "Darla" are close in relation, when really the only thing close are the letters used. But, the second blaring issue, which is also the most important one, is the fact that the Fragmentary Annals are not considered a legitimate contemporary source, which gives many historians who still doubt his existence a very good reason to be suspicious of their legitimacy and their accuracy.

But, even if we admit that the events given to this Ragnall character are historically accurate, and then admit further that these particular events could have been the basis for the overall Ragnar legend, then it would still have to be admitted that the person the legend was based off did not have the right name...

and many historians and scholars who do believe of his existence do not want to concede that because of how ingrained Ragnar Lothbrok's stories are into our own culture.

See the issue?

But, putting their personal biases aside, is it possible that "Ragnall" and "Lothbrok" could have been the same person? Is it possible that two individuals were combined, both in time and in stories, in order to garner the heroic figure of Ragnar Lothbrok as we understand him today?

With all the information provided above as seen in particular moments of ancient texts, the only reasonable regard historians can give to the figure of "Ragnar Lothbrok" is the fact that "Ragnall" and "Lothbrok" were both the same person, but given an overall name in order to garner a larger-than-life character told for future generations in order to instill into future Viking children a pride in their cultural history and to teach them of the strength of their culture and ways of life.

There is an article entitled Lothbrok in The Irish Annals, where R. W. McTurk approached this very issue from an interesting viewpoint: he took a look at all the statements made in all of these surrounding sources and postulated as to what types of assumptions might have been made about those particular statements that have brought us to accept a historical figure named Ragnar Lothbrok who was ultimately a member of the Danish royal family.

Many scholars believe it is not necessary for Lothbrok's existence to have been royal in order for his existence to have been real and historical, though many other scholars argue that part of the incredible story of Lothbrok is the fact that he did not fall onto his family's wealth and prominence to make a name for himself but, instead, did it himself.

However, without postulating about any requirements that might be "necessary" for Lothbrok's origin story, there are seven basic assumptions that have been made from several lines of texts that lack situational foundation other than intelligent theorizing of scholars that "Ragnall Lothbrok" and "Ragnar Lothbrok" are, in fact, the same person:

1. We have to assume that Adam of Bremen was actually right in giving the name "Lodparchus" as Ivar's father in the late 9th-century.

2. We have to assume that a 12th-century Irish source, entitled The War of the Gaedhil with the Gaill, is right in stating that Halfdan of Dublin was the son of Ragnall, and that this is the same Ragnall who appears in the Fragmentary Annals of Ireland.

3. We have to assume that the Anglo-Saxon Chronicle is right in stating within its walls of texts that an unnamed brother, who was eventually called "Ubbe" in sources that came later, was killed in 878 in England, even though there is a contradictory statement by Aethelweard that has a very different interpretation and reading for this same death event.

4. We also have to assume that the chronicle of Aethelweard is still wrong in also stating that Halfdan was killed in 878 in England, because without that death date it could be proven that Halfdan of Dublin was a completely different person from Halfdan, the brother of Ivar.

5. Alongside all of this assuming of the Halfdans, we also have to assume that this "Ivar" was the exact same person that Adam of Bremen talked of, and all while keeping in mind that Aethelweard's chronicle would imply the existence of two Ivars in this British Isles

area at the same time (if that part of Aethelweard's chronicle is correct).

6. We have to also assume that the idea of "Lothbroka" being a feminine derivative and, therefore, placing Ragnar Lothbrok as a female is also false.

7. Then, we also have to assume that if Ari (who is the earliest author that mentions "Ragnar Lothbrok") is considered a reliable source of information, that Halfdan of Dublin was also the same person as Halfdan, the brother of Sigifrid, who appears multiple times in the Annals of Fulda during the year 873 (even though many chronological issues in years and dates would mess up Ari's pre-established genealogies and familial trees).

If we settle the boggling of our minds long enough, we see that numbers one through six are crucial to identifying that "Ragnall" and "Lothbrok" are the same person. If we take a deep breath, we will also see that seven is also necessary if it is to be theorized that any information given by the first ever writer of Ragnar Lothbrok (Ari) is anywhere near accurate. But, if any one of the first six items are false, then the case for "Ragnall Lothbrok" falls to pieces.

Even with all this postulation and theorization, it can be easier (after outlining all of this stuff) to see why historians and scholars alike struggle to identify whether Ragnar Lothbrok truly did live. Since all of the above outlined attempts to find a physical and historical figure to suit the ideals we have about Ragnar Lothbrok all fail in some way, shape, or form, it is understandable as to why the sources that combine "Ragnall" and "Lothbrok" are met with the utmost skepticism within the community.

Thus, with all of this taken into consideration, it is still a mystery as to whether Ragnar Lothbrok truly did exist.

If we take it one step further and state that there is some sort of historical basis for Ragnar Lothbrok, and we have simply not found it yet, then it is very likely that Ragnar Lothbrok is the outcome of combining multiple individuals into one single character that houses attributes from all of its combined true-to-life individuals. It has already been proven that Ragnar Lothbrok's "father", Sigurd Ring, is actually the combination of two different men who fought bravely and hard against one another for the Danish throne in 814 (those two men, by the way, are "Sigifridus" and "Anulo", meaning "Sigurd" and "Ring", respectively).

But, just because Lothbrok's "father" was a composite does not necessary mean that he is.

Ragnar Lothbrok's true existence, while still highly debated upon, does not make the stories that surround him any less intriguing, entertaining, and interesting. Sometimes the greater purpose is not the existence of a character, but the lessons a person can learn from the "life" of that character.

Whatever you choose to believe, know this: Ragnar Lothbrok was strong, capable, ruthless, and the leader of his Viking people. He understood their way of life, how to garner favor and trust within his people and, by all definitions of how we define a "ruler", understood what it took in order to rule his community.

That much will never be debated.

Conclusion

Thanks again for taking the time to read this book!

You should now have a good understanding of Ragnar Lothbrok and the incredible life he lived as a Viking warrior!

If you enjoyed this book, please take the time to leave me a review on Amazon. I appreciate your honest feedback, and it really helps me to continue producing high quality books

CPSIA information can be obtained
at www.ICGtesting.com
Printed in the USA
BVHW091710301120
594477BV00011B/2186